ASIA

A TRUE BOOK

by
David Petersen

Children's Press®

A Division of Grolier Publishing

New York London Hong Kong Sydney
Danbury, Connecticut

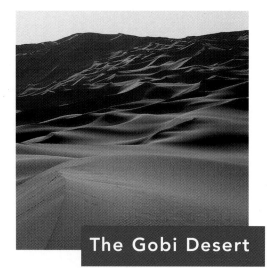

The Gobi Desert

Reading Consultant
Linda Cornwell
Learning Resource Consultant
Indiana Department of
Education

Visit Children's Press on the Internet at:
http://publishing.grolier.com

Library of Congress Cataloging-in-Publication Data

Petersen, David, 1946–
    Asia / by David Petersen.
        p.   cm. — (A True book)
    Includes bibliographical references and index.
    Summary: A brief overview of the geography, wildlife, history, and
people of Asia.
    ISBN 0–516–20764–4 (lib. bdg.)   0-516-26371-4 (pbk.)
    1. Asia—Juvenile literature. [1. Asia.] I. Title. II. Series.
DS5.P4 1998
950—dc21
                                               97–35687
                                                  CIP
                                                  AC

Contents

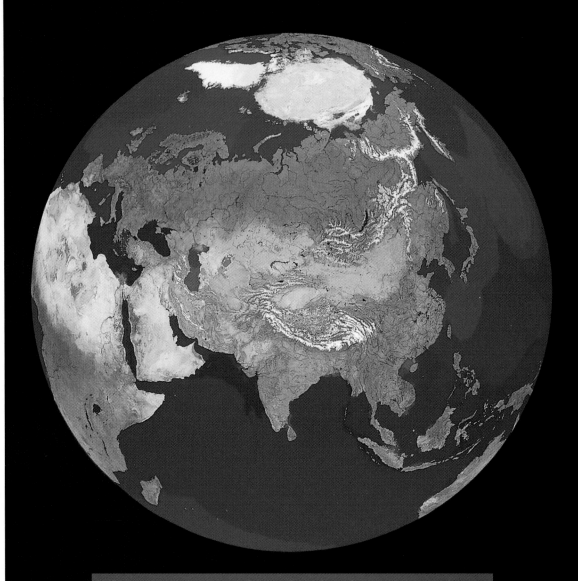

This picture, taken high above Earth, shows Asia and parts of the neighboring continents. The tan areas on the Arabian Peninsula and in central Asia are desert regions. The white areas are high, snowcapped mountains.

Continent in the Middle

Asia is the biggest of the world's seven continents. It covers about a third of Earth's land mass—about 17 million square miles (44 million square kilometers).

In the northeast, the Bering Strait, a narrow stretch of water only 56 miles (90 kilometers) wide, separates Asia from the North American continent. And the islands of Southeast Asia reach almost to the continent of Australia.

In the northwest, Asia is separated from Europe by the Ural Mountains. Western Asia also touches the continent of Africa. The Arabian Peninsula in Asia borders Egypt in Africa.

Asia is truly the continent in the middle.

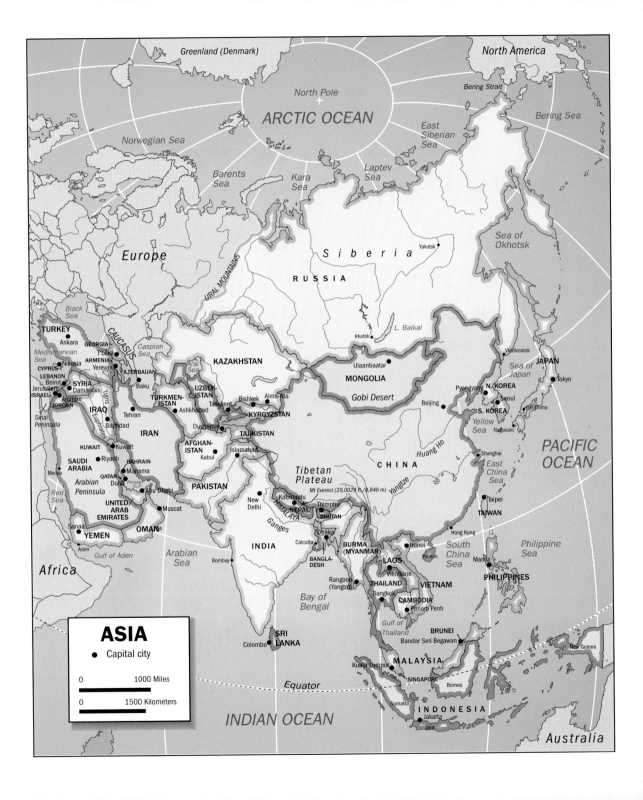

Asia has forty-nine independent nations. The three biggest in area and population are Russia in the north, China in the east, and India in the south.

The Asian island nations of Japan, Taiwan, and the Philippines lie off the east coast of China. The Pacific Ocean splashes against the eastern shores of these islands. South of the Philippines, in Southeast Asia, a string of islands makes up the nation of Indonesia.

The plume of smoke in this satellite picture is rising from a volcano near Kagoshima, Japan.

The vast continent of Asia stretches from the Indian Ocean in the south to the icy Arctic Ocean in the north.

Asian Highs and Lows

In south-central Asia, between India and China, stand the massive Himalaya mountains. The snowcapped peak of Mount Everest is the highest point on Earth at 29,029 feet (8,848 meters).

The lowest place on Earth, the Dead Sea, lies west of the

Mount Everest, on the border of Nepal and Tibet, is the highest mountain on Earth.

Himalaya at the border between Jordan and Israel. The Dead Sea is a saltwater lake whose shoreline is 1,296 feet (395 m) below sea level.

The Dead Sea is the saltiest body of water on Earth. There is so much salt in the water that people float easily.

Between the soaring Himalaya and the sunken Dead Sea sprawls the land-locked Caspian Sea. With a surface area of 143,200 square miles (371,000 sq. km), this big salty sea is the world's largest lake.

The Caspian Sea is the largest lake in the world.

Nature's Wonderland

Asia is home to many kinds of animals. In the arctic lands of northern Siberia, reindeer survive by eating tiny plants called lichens. Lichens are the only plants that are plentiful in this icy place. The reindeer have thick fur coats to keep them warm and large hooves for walking on snow.

Many reindeer live in northern Siberia (below). They eat lichens (right) to survive.

The snow leopard's white coat blends in with its snowy surroundings.

High in the Himalaya, the snow leopard's white coat blends in with the snow and rocks of its mountain home. Its coloring makes the snow leopard difficult to see as it hunts wild sheep and other animals.

In Southeast Asia and India, elephants eat the leaves and branches of the trees that grow in the forests where they live. To gather their tree-top food, elephants have long, flexible trunks.

The elephant's long trunk allows it to reach high leaves.

In western Asia, out on the Arabian Peninsula, camels live in the dry, hot desert. Camels can survive in this harsh environment because they have developed the ability to go days or weeks without food or water.

Camels survive in the Arabian Desert because they can go many days without food and water.

Long-haired yaks are common in Tibet.

The long-haired yak wanders over the Tibetan Plateau. The peaceful orangutan and

An orangutan mother cuddles her baby (top). This Komodo dragon (middle) is 10 feet (3 m) long. A panda eats bamboo (bottom).

Asia Fast Facts

Area 17,297,000 square miles (44,799,000 sq. km)

Highest point Mount Everest, Tibet and Nepal: 29,029 feet (8,848 m)

Lowest point Dead Sea, Israel and Jordan: 1,296 feet (395 m) below sea level

Longest River Yangtze, China: 3,195 miles (6,300 km)

Largest Lake Caspian Sea: 143,250 square miles (371,000 sq. km)

Number of independent nations 49

Population 3.5 billion

To Find Out More

Here are some additional resources to help you learn more about the continent of Asia:

 **Books**

Conklin, Paul. **Land of Yesterday, Land of Tomorrow: Discovering Chinese Central Asia.** Cobblehill Books/Dutton, 1992.

Heinrichs, Ann. **China.** Children's Press, 1997.

Heinrichs, Ann. **Japan.** Children's Press, 1997.

Honeyman, Susannah. **Saudi Arabia.** Raintree Steck-Vaughn, 1995.

Ingpen, Robert. **Folk Tales and Fables of Asia and Australia.** Chelsea House, 1994.

Major, John S. **The Silk Route: 7,000 Miles of History.** HarperCollins, 1995.

McLoone, Margo. **Women Explorers in Asia.** Capstone Press, 1997.

Noonan, Jon. **Marco Polo.** Macmillan International, 1993.

Rigg, Jonathan. **Southeast Asia.** Raintree Steck-Vaughn, 1995.

Wilkinson, Philip. **The Magical East: Mysterious Places.** Chelsea House, 1994.

Organizations and Online Sites

Asia on RootsWorld
http://www.rootsworld. com/rw/asia.html
Information about Asian music.

Asian Arts
http://www.asianart.com/
Articles and photographs of old and new art from all parts of Asia.

Asian Mall Kid's Corner
http://www.asianmall.com/ kids/
Links to lots of sites about Asia especially for kids.

AskAsia
http://www.askasia.org/
Lots of information about Asia. Check out the adult-free zone for information just for kids.

INTELLiCast: Asia Weather
http://www.intellicast.com/ weather/asia/
Forecasts and weather information for Asia.

Kids Web Japan
http://www.jinjapan.org/ kidsweb/index.html
Information about Japan especially for kids.

Important Words

agriculture farming and raising livestock

continent one of the seven large land masses of the earth

geography the study of Earth's surface features and dimensions

habitat the natural environment of a plant or animal

lichens plants made up of an algae and a fungus

nomadic wandering

orangutan a large ape that lives in rain forests

strait a narrow passage connecting two large bodies of water

yak a wild ox

the toothy Komodo dragon (a huge lizard) make their homes in the jungles of Indonesia. The giant panda munches on bamboo leaves in China's mountain forests.

Because of its great size and variety of habitats, Asia has been a natural wonderland for millions of years. But today, human activity is rapidly destroying natural habitats in Asia and elsewhere.

The Many Faces of Asia

About 3.5 billion people live in Asia, making it the most populated continent. The first humans to occupy Asia walked over from Africa about a million years ago. By twenty thousand years ago, people had spread throughout the giant continent. Asian people come from so many different

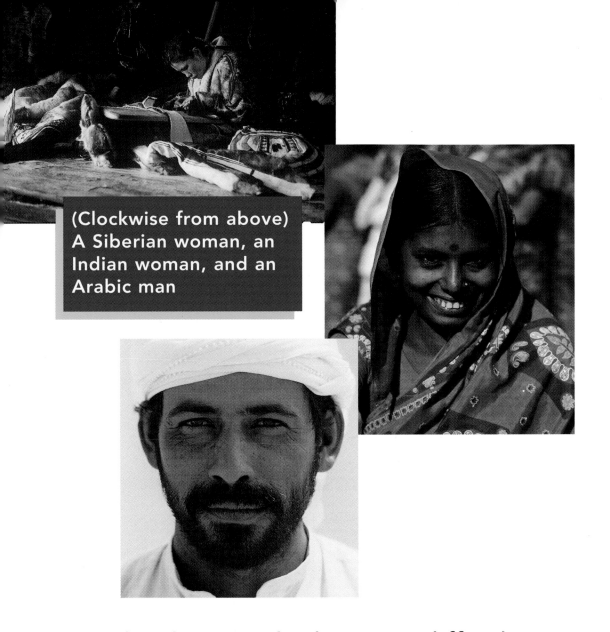

(Clockwise from above)
A Siberian woman, an
Indian woman, and an
Arabic man

backgrounds that it is difficult
to separate them into just a
few groups.

Asiatic people occupy central and eastern Asia. Arabic people live in southwestern Asia. Indian people live in India and the surrounding countries of southern Asia. Caucasians occupy northwestern Asia.

Each of these four basic types can be subdivided into smaller ethnic groups. People in an ethnic group share the same ancestry, language, culture, and religion. An ethnic

(Clockwise from top left) Japanese school-children, a Turkish woman, and an Inner Mongolian woman

group may be large or small, and its members may live in more than one country.

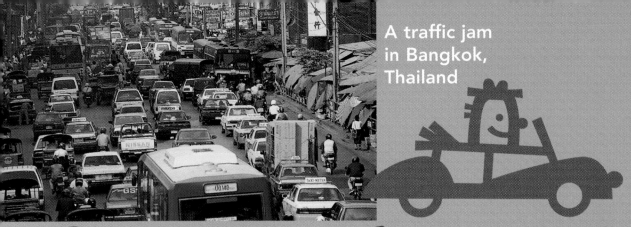

A traffic jam in Bangkok, Thailand

Getting Around

In Asia's many crowded cities, traffic jams are common. In China, many people bicycle to work. Japan is known for its fantastic train system. But sometimes, so many people need to get on a train, the conductors have to shove people through the doors. In Mongolia, far from the big cities, horses or motorcycles are used to cross the plains. In the dry deserts of Mongolia and Arabia, hardy camels are used to get around.

Camels are used to cross the Arabian Desert

Civilization's Cradle

For thousands of years, all the people of Asia were nomadic hunters and gatherers. They did not live in one area for very long. They followed the animals they hunted or moved where the wild plants they ate grew best.

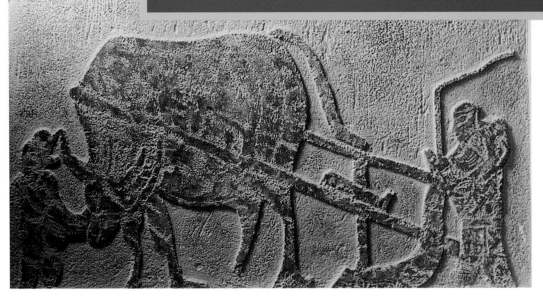

Then, about ten thousand years ago, people began farming. This meant that they could grow the food they needed. Agriculture began in southwest Asia in an area called the

Many Asian people still make a living on farms. These steplike hillsides in China are used to grow rice.

Fertile Crescent, which lies between the Persian Gulf and the Mediterranean Sea.

By six thousand years ago, Asians started keeping sheep, goats, pigs, horses, cows, and other animals on farms. People could now stay in one place and produce everything they needed for food, clothing, and shelter.

Agriculture made life easier in Asia, and the human population began to grow very rapidly. Camps became farming villages. Villages became cities. By five thousand years ago, Asia had developed the world's first civilizations with laws, religions, trade, politics . . . and warfare.

A Warrior's World

The nation of Mongolia lies in south-central Asia. Its broad grassy plains, called steppes, provide the perfect habitat for wild horses. The Mongols were the world's first horsemen.

Before they learned to ride horses, the Mongols were a peaceful people. They roamed

Wild horses on a
Mongolian plain

the plains tending their animals. But with the newfound
speed, power, and mobility of
horses, they became ruthless
warriors. No place on the Asian
continent was safe from
Mongol raiders on horseback.

The most famous Mongol ruler was Genghis Khan, a title that means "universal ruler." His original name was Temüjin, which means "ironworker." He was born about 1162. When Temüjin was about thirteen years old, his father was killed, forcing the boy to take on adult responsibilities.

The boy became a man, and the man became a leader. Under Temüjin, the many independent Mongol tribes were

This detail of an illustration made in 1590 shows Genghis Khan's warriors during a battle.

united into one huge army on horseback. During the 1200s, the Mongols controlled all of Asia and parts of Europe.

Genghis Khan died in 1227, but his sons and grandsons carried on. By 1280, the Mongols had built the world's largest land empire. Along the way, millions of people were killed, making the rule of the Mongols one of the bloodiest periods in Asian history.

Today, Mongolia is a peaceful nation. About half of its 2.3 million people work as herders and live in traditional round tents called *yurts*, just like the

Many Mongolians live in traditional round tents called yurts.

one in which Genghis Khan was born. A yurt is a sturdy, cozy tent made of felt. It can be taken down quickly and moved from one place to another to follow the livestock.

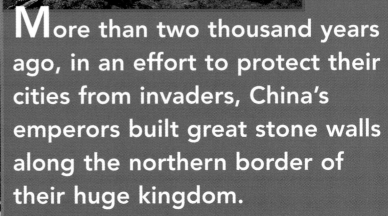

The Great Wall

More than two thousand years ago, in an effort to protect their cities from invaders, China's emperors built great stone walls along the northern border of their huge kingdom.

The Great Wall of China was entirely built by hand and took hundreds of years to complete. It's about 4,000 miles (6,400 km) long, making it the largest structure ever built by humans. In places it is as high as 35 feet (11 m) and as wide as 25 feet (7.6 m). Much of the Great Wall still stands today. It is a popular tourist attraction.

Asia Now

Modern Asia is home to more than 3.5 billion people—more than half of all the humans on Earth! Spread evenly across the continent, that would average 205 people per square mile (79 per sq. km).

But much of Asia—including Arctic Siberia and the Arabian

Few people can live in the harsh conditions of Siberia (top) and the Gobi Desert (bottom).

The beautiful city of Hong Kong, located on China's south coast, is an important center for trade around the world. After 99 years of British control, Hong Kong was returned to China in 1997.

and Gobi deserts—is too cold or too dry for people to live there. As a result, millions of Asians live in crowded cities with populations of thousands of persons per square mile.

Many other Asians still follow traditional agricultural lifestyles. Millions make their living as farmers and herders. Millions of others live along rivers and seacoasts where fish are plentiful.

Asia is a land filled with wonder, mystery, and hope. It has the highest mountains, the lowest seas, and is home to a tremendous variety of people. You could spend a lifetime exploring Asia

Many Asians live in rural areas such as the mountain village of Namche Bazaar. Namche Bazaar has become a popular spot for tourists visiting the Mount Everest region.

without discovering all this fantastic continent has to offer.

Meet the Author

As a military pilot, David Petersen visited Japan, Okinawa, Korea, the Philippines, and other Asian nations. Today, he lives in Colorado in a cabin he built himself. He enjoys reading, writing, hiking, camping, and dogs. His "grown-up" books include *Among the Elk* (North-land) and *A Hunter's Heart* (Henry Holt). Mr. Petersen has written many other books on geography for Children's Press, including True Books on all the continents.

Index